I0471629

BUSINESS ENGLISH FOR INVESTORS

Execu Speak
DICTIONARY™

Because business *is* another language.

Translating from ExecuSpeak, the language of business, into something useful and understandable no longer requires a team of attorneys or an advanced degree.

Compiled and edited by
Carol Heiberger

Contributor: Karen L. Jett

www.execuspeakdictionary.com

ExecuSpeak Dictionary^{tm}

Business English for Investors

Copyright 2012 Winter Babel, LLC. All rights reserved. Printed in the United States of America. No part of this book may be used or reproduced in any manner whatsoever without written permission except in the case of reprints in the context of review. For information, write Carol Heiberger, 1636 Waverly Street, Philadelphia, PA 19146.

Lulu Print Edition

ISBN #: 978-1-105-80511-0

www.ExecuSpeakDictionary.com

Cover Design and Logo by Bondepus

ATTENTION: SCHOOLS & BUSINESSES

The ExecuSpeak Dictionary^{tm} is available at quantity discounts with bulk purchase for education, business, or sales promotional use. For information, contact Carol Heiberger at carol@execuspeakdictionary.com.

Dedicated to everyone who has been frustrated or
confused by American business English.

TABLE OF CONTENTS

About the Author

Carol Heiberger is an independent consultant specializing in business creation. She is an experienced interim executive and project manager of large-scale, multi-location projects. Her industry experience includes positions with the Ford Motor Company, Bell Atlantic, a start-up CATV/ISP, and a large energy utility.

This experience has given her expertise in strategic planning, new business development, marketing, and finance with large complex organizations, small entrepreneurial groups, and domestic and international markets. Carol's approach is simple: she creates effective teams by translating across functions and disciplines with a collaborative and hands-on leadership style.

Carol also has strong affiliations with educational institutions in Philadelphia. She has taught both degree-seeking graduate students and knowledge-seeking adults of all ages and walks of life.

Execuspeak Dictionary was born of Carol's insights gained over her diverse 30-year career. She earned her MBA from Wharton.

About the Contributor

Karen L. Jett, CMA (Certified Management Accountant), of Jett Excellence, works with small business owners who want a strategic advantage to grow their business or practice. She created an innovative Strategic Plan-ting Workshop where, in one day, entrepreneurs create a strategic plan for their business using a process similar to those used by larger organizations.

With over two decades of accounting and business leadership experience, Karen brings a unique business perspective to the table. She understands the operational and financial challenges businesspeople face on a daily basis.

Introduction

The dictionary's website (www.execuspeakdictionary.com) is your source of up to date information concerning books, products, news, programs. Facebook and Twitter allow users to connect, to follow, and to receive a word a day.

Consider purchasing the complete ExecuSpeak Dictionary with over 500 business terms that are defined in plain English and then used in a sentence. In the paper version, there are 18 subject matter indexes plus an alphabetical index to ease navigation.

About pronunciation: The only words for which pronunciation is provided are acronyms that have become words, such as GIGO (pronounced gee-gow). All other acronyms are pronounced letter by letter.

Carol Heiberger

NUMERICS

401(K)

A retirement savings plan offered by employers that has tax advantages for employees.

Usage: The young employees didn't understand the value of the 401(k) because the concept of retirement was hard for them to grasp.

403(B)

A retirement savings plan for staff and faculty who work for not-for-profit and educational institutions.

Usage: A 403(b) is similar to a 401(k) except it is for educators instead of private company employees.

A

Accredited Investor

Term defined by US securities law to describe someone who earns at least $200,000 per year or has at least $1 million in net worth and is interested in making certain types of risky investments.

Usage: The entrepreneur was looking for accredited investors so he could raise the funds to expand his business.

Accretive

An acquisition that will increase the earnings per share (EPS) calculation for the company that makes the purchase.

Usage: The CEO proudly told the financial analysts that the deal would be accretive.

Acquisition

The purchase of one company or some of its divisions by another company.

Usage: The acquisition of the small company was motivated by the larger company's need for new products and services.

Actuals

The financial or numerical data that describes what happened in the past. Compares to the budget.

Usage: The manager looked at the budget vs. actuals report that was published at the end of each quarter.

Affiliate Transactions

Business activity between two or more business entities that are controlled, owned by, or managed by a single parent corporation. Ownership of 5% or more generally triggers affiliate transaction considerations.

Usage: Sometimes affiliate transactions are governed by special laws or accounting rules.

Aggressive

An estimate, financial goal, or investment position that is risky or not cautious. Opposite of conservative.

Usage: Sometimes an aggressive approach to stock picking is akin to gambling.

Angel Investor

An individual who provides money, or start-up capital, to help a new business to get started.

Usage: New entrepreneurs dream of finding an angel investor, but it's very difficult.

Annual Review

A review of a firm's financial statements by an outside company that is not as thorough as an audit.

Usage: Many small companies get an annual review because it is cheaper than an audit.

Anti-Trust

Body of law that describes agreements and practices that restrain trade.

Usage: Companies that get together to set prices are violating anti-trust laws.

Asset

An object or right that results from past events and is expected to create future economic benefits.

Usage: Manufacturing equipment is an asset that creates products that will be sold for profit.

Asset Class

A grouping of investments, securities, or assets that share similar qualities, levels of risk, or industrial sectors.

Usage: Some analysts claim that there are only four asset classes—real estate, stocks, bonds, and cash—while others use different categories.

Audit

A thorough review of a company's financial statements, including a comment on conformance to generally accepted accounting principles (GAAP). (But the word is frequently used to refer to a more general review.)

Usage: All publicly traded companies are required to have an annual audit.

B

B2B

Business to Business. Often-used abbreviation of the business model in which one company sells to other companies (as compared to B2C, selling to consumers).

Usage: The B2B marketing programs included ads in business periodicals.

B2C

Business to Consumer. Often-used abbreviation of the business model in which one company sells to consumers or individuals (as compared to B2B, selling to businesses).

Usage: The B2C marketing program included television advertising.

Bear

Investor or commentator who thinks that market value will go down. Pessimist. Opposite of a bull.

Usage: The investment adviser described himself as a bear and suggested that stocks might lose value over the next few weeks.

Bearish

Negative in outlook. Refers to Wall Street "bears." Opposite of bullish.

Usage: The financial commentator had a bearish outlook on the market.

Benchmark

A product, service, or process that is considered the best in its class.

Usage: Selecting an appropriate benchmark is an important step in improving service levels.

Best Practices

Techniques, methods, incentives, policies, behaviors, and systems that perform a particular function well.

Usage: According to best practices research, competitive intelligence is a continuous process that continues for the life of the product.

Beta

A statistical measure of a company's stock volatility, or variability, in relationship to the rest of the stocks in the stock market.

Usage: A high beta stock is one with wide swings in price from day to day or week to week.

Bond

An agreement between two parties to exchange cash now for cash plus interest at a later date.

Usage: A bond is a way for a company to access cash without a bank loan.

BRIC

A collective name for Brazil, Russia, India, and China. Pronounced as brik.

Usage: The financial analyst's report concentrated on the BRIC economies.

Bull

Investor or commentator who thinks that market value will go up. Optimist. Opposite of a bear.

Usage: The Wall Street bull thought that the trends were good for the investment community.

Bullish

Positive in outlook on the value of investments.

Usage: We were pleased that the market commentator was bullish on the stock we had just bought.

C

Capital Intensive

A business, product, or service that is highly dependent on equipment or capital investment. Compares to labor intensive.

Usage: The telecommunications business is highly capital intensive because of the amount of money required to purchase and install switches, transmission media, and monitoring equipment.

Cash Cow

A description of a product at the point in the product life cycle where revenues are strong and selling expenses are low.

Usage: A cash cow is frequently in the mature product life cycle stage.

C-Level

Business managers and executives with titles that being with the word Chief, such as Chief Executive Officer (CEO), Chief Financial Officer (CFO), Chief Technology Officer (CTO), and Chief Information Officer (CIO).

Usage: The marketing program was designed to get the attention of C-level executives.

Close

The end of a day's trading on the NYSE or the NASDAQ.

Usage: The Dow was up 39 points at the close.

Collateral

The assets that a borrower pledges to a lender when taking out a loan.

Usage: If the borrower does not repay the loan, then the collateral becomes the property of the lender.

Common Stock

A method for selling ownership rights of a business.

Usage: Common stock gives holders the right to vote on important company issues.

Conservative

An estimate, financial goal, or investment position that is risk-averse or cautious. Opposite of aggressive.

Usage: A conservative estimate of costs implies that the expected costs will actually be lower than stated.

Continuous Improvement

The never-ending effort to expose and eliminate root causes of problems.

Usage: As a result of continuous improvement, the processes were getting more and more efficient every year.

Convergence

The coming together of two or more things.

Usage: There appears to be a convergence in the capabilities of cell phones and computers.

Correlation

The extent or degree of statistical association among two or more variables.

Usage: Just because there is a correlation between two events doesn't mean that one caused the other.

Cost Center

A logical subdivision of the company that is responsible for controlling only costs. Opposite of a revenue center.

Usage: The production department is a cost center.

D

Direct Deposit

An electronic deposit from one bank account to another.

Usage: Direct deposit eliminates the need to print a paper check.

Dividend

A payment to stockholders that represents a share of the profits.

Usage: Growth companies frequently do not pay dividends; instead they invest the money in future growth opportunitie

E

Earnings Per Share

Net income less preferred dividends divided by the number of shares of outstanding stock. Also referred to as EPS.

Usage: The CEO's bonus was based on growth in EPS.

EBITDA

Earnings Before Interest, Taxes, Depreciation, and Amortization. Pronounced as ee-bit-da. A line on the income statement.

Usage: EBITDA is an indicator of profitability and cash flow.

Equity

Total assets less total liabilities. Owner's equity or capital is usually a large percentage of total equity. Everything owned after debt is subtracted.

Usage: Equity is also frequently called net assets.

Exit Strategy

The plan for getting out of an investment or getting one's money back after it has been invested.

Usage: The exit strategy, for venture capital investors, is to sell their shares on the stock exchange (also known as taking a company public).

F

FASB

Financial Accounting Standards Board. Pronounced faz-bee. Its primary purpose is to develop generally accepted accounting principles (GAAP).

Usage: The FASB regularly issues new accounting standards for US companies to follow.

Fed

United States Federal Reserve System; also called the Federal Reserve. The central banking system of the US government. The leadership is appointed by the president and confirmed by the Senate.

Usage: The Fed is responsible for supervising and regulating US banks as well as providing services to banks and the government.

Financial Analysis

Evaluation and assessment of monetary resources associated with a business or a business opportunity.

Usage: The results of the financial analysis helped the manager understand how much money had to be spent and how long it might take for revenues to exceed costs.

Financial Risk

The likelihood of loss or less-than-expected returns. Also refers to the potential for losing money.

Usage: Gamblers are willing to take more financial risk than cautious spenders.

FINRA

Financial INdustry Regulatory Authority. Pronounced fin-rah. An independent regulator for all securities firms doing business in the United States, dedicated to investor protection and market integrity.

Usage: FINRA responsibilities include enforcing industry and federal securities laws.

Fiscal Year

The 12-month period used to calculate financial statements. It may not be the same as a calendar year.

Usage: The fiscal year ran from July 1 to June 30 for the company that did most of its business at Christmas.

Forecast

A financial projection based on information from the recent past, future plans, and expectations.

Usage: A forecast in the last quarter showed that if no changes were made, budget numbers would not be met.

Foreign

Describing operations that take place in a country other than the one in which the business is headquartered. Opposite of domestic.

Usage: The Chinese company's office in New York City was included in their report outlining their foreign offices.

Fungible

Interchangeable with other individual goods or assets of the same type.

Usage: Money is fungible. Once funds are placed into a common account it is not possible to separate the sources of the money.

Futureproof

A technology or strategy that will not become obsolete or outdated in the foreseeable future.

Usage: Fiber is considered to be a futureproof technology because its transmission capacity is limitless.

FX

Foreign Exchange. The buying and selling of currency and money between countries. FX markets are also called ForEx.

Usage: The FX trader was closely watching relationship between the Euro and the US dollar.

G

GAAP

Generally Accepted Accounting Principles. Pronounced gap. Rules and standards for preparing financial statements that are issued by the AICPA.

Usage: Financial statements of US-based companies must comply with GAAP so that analysts can compare information between companies.

Gain

Incidental income that does not relate to normal business operations or investments by owners. Also the opposite of loss.

Usage: The sale of a piece of production equipment for more than its book value results in a gain.

Going Concern

Describes a company that is expected to continue operating now and in the future, since it has all the resources it needs to remain in business.

Usage: Accountants frequently give "going concern" opinions.

Goodwill

A type of intangible asset that results from purchasing a company for more than the fair value of its assets and liabilities.

Usage: Because Alpha Co. paid $5 million more than fair value for Beta Corp., it now has $5 million of goodwill on its balance sheet.

Gross Profit

Sales revenue less the direct costs associated with creating what was sold. The profit that is available to cover other operating expenses.

Usage: The gross profit from selling a book is the difference between what the book sold for and the price the bookstore paid for it.

H

High Net Worth

Description of people with money, property, and other assets that greatly exceed their level of debt.

Usage: The exact amount of money that makes someone a high net worth individual may vary by bank or investment adviser.

Human Capital

People and all the good things that come with them.

Usage: Some companies refer to the special skills and capabilities of their employees as human capital.

Hurdle Rate

The minimum return on investment acceptable for a project to be considered.

Usage: The project was turned down because its expected return was less than the hurdle rate.

I

Income Statement

A financial statement that lists the revenues and expenses for a period of time. Also called profit and loss statement.

Usage: The CFO was reading the income statement to prepare for his meetings.

Insider

In formal terms, someone who has special, non-public knowledge about plans and events that might have an impact on the price of a stock.

Usage: The CEO's wife was accused of insider trading because she used her knowledge of his schedule to trade stock in his company.

Investable Assets

Cash and securities that can be spent, saved, or invested. Opposite of assets that are not liquid such as homes, artwork, and jewelry.

Usage: The stockbroker asked about the prospective client's investable assets.

J

JV

Joint Venture. A business structure whereby two or more individuals or entities agree to work together for a single project.

Usage: Sometimes a JV is just a teaming arrangement between two companies.

K

Kaizen

A Japanese concept that refers to continuous improvement efforts.

Usage: Using the principles of kaizen, we focused on reducing production costs by 3% year after year for each of the past five years.

L

Labor Intensive

A business, product, or service that is highly dependent on the work efforts of people. Compares to capital intensive.

Usage: A housecleaning business is labor intensive because people are needed to dust, mop, and vacuum.

Liability

An obligation that results from an event that occurred in the past. The obligation may be settled by paying cash, transferring an asset, or providing a service.

Usage: Money borrowed from the bank is a liability, as it will need to be repaid.

Line Of Credit

A loan that permits the borrower to borrow or repay money as cash flow allows. Abbreviated as LOC.

Usage: The line of credit was used to fund payroll when cash was not available

Liquid Asset

An asset such as a stock, bond, or a savings account that can be converted into cash within a very short period of time.

Usage: Real estate is not considered a liquid asset since it might take some time to find a buyer.

Long-Term Liability

A liability that is payable more than 12 months into the future. Opposite of current liability.

Usage: A 15-year traditional mortgage is both a current liability and a long-term liability.

Loss

The outcome when expenses exceed revenues. The value of an asset when it is sold for less than the amount paid. Opposite of a gain.

Usage: The homeowners sold their house at a loss.

M

Management Control

The words, actions, and policies of the management team that can affect events.

Usage: Weather events are outside of management control.

Market Share

The percent of the potential customers that are actually purchasing a specific product or service.

Usage: The product manager's new marketing plan was designed to increase market share.

Market Value

The amount of money for which an asset could be sold in the open market.

Usage: The market value of an asset is rarely the same as book value.

Matures

Becomes due; refers to a note or other debt instrument.

Usage: When a note payable matures, the company must pay out the principal payment due.

Measurable

Something that can be measured or tracked.

Usage: The manager's performance review was based on measurable goals.

Merger

The combining of two separate companies or divisions.

Usage: A merger is akin to a marriage between business entities.

Merger Of Equals

The combining of two companies that are of the same size and strength.

Usage: A merger of equals implies that neither acquired or purchased the other.

MOU

Memorandum of Understanding. Similar to a Letter of Intent (LOI), the MOU describes the principles of a future agreement.

Usage: An MOU is frequently the first documented step in a Joint Venture.

N

Negative Growth

The opposite of positive growth. Might be a decline.

Usage: The economy caused the company to have negative growth. Revenues were down.

Net Income

All income less all expenses including taxes. Sometimes referred to as profit. Accountants distinguish between pre-tax and after-tax net income.

Usage: Net income for the year was down as a result of the tax increase.

O

Open

The beginning of a day's trading on the NYSE or the NASDAQ.

Usage: The Dow was up 15 points at the open.

Operating Income

Operating revenues less all operating expenses except income taxes and interest. Sometimes referred to as EBIT (Earnings Before Interest and Taxes).

Usage: The financial analysts were examining the changes in operating income from year to year.

Opex

OPerating EXpenses. Those expenses in a financial statement that represent the money spent by the business.

Usage: The managers were trying to figure out how to decrease opex and increase profits.

OPM

Other People's Money. Bank or personal loans, venture capital, investment, or grants that might be made available to a business.

Usage: The business owner was looking for OPM instead of putting his own money at risk.

Opportunity Cost

The cost of forgoing one opportunity in favor of another. A means of describing the tradeoff between options.

Usage: For the student, the opportunity cost associated with going to the movies was the homework that would not get done that evening.

Overweight

Circumstance where the portfolio has too much of one asset and is out of balance. Opposite of underweight.

Usage: The analyst said he was overweight stocks, implying that he would not purchase any more.

Owner's Equity

The ownership transactions of a business that represent the owner's claims. May be contributed, as in capital stock, or earned, as in retained earnings.

Usage: Capital is a type of equity, so it is sometimes referred to as owner's equity.

P

P&L

Profit and Loss (Statement). The portion of a financial analysis that identifies all sources of revenues and expenses and calculates profit.

Usage: The vice-president had P&L responsibility for his department.

Par Value

The stated or face value of a stock or bond.

Usage: The market value and par value of stock are usually different.

Parent Company

The company that owns the stock of another company or controls its business activities.

Usage: Altria is the parent company of Philip Morris USA.

Partnership Agreement

The legal document that describes the terms and conditions of a partnership.

Usage: According to the partnership agreement, each of the four partners would get 25% of the profits.

Planning Assumption

Assumptions made in order to plan for the (unknown) future.

Usage: When a planning assumption proves to be untrue, it's time to revisit the plan.

Preferred Stock

A method for selling ownership rights of a business while limiting active participation in the company.

Usage: Preferred stock gives holders the right to receive dividends before common stockholders.

Pro Forma Financial Statement

Financial statement prepared using budgeted or forecasted numbers.

Usage: After completing the budget, we can create pro forma financial statements to see what the net income might be.

Profit

The outcome when revenues exceed expenses. Opposite of a loss.

Usage: The entrepreneur's goal was to make a profit by the end of the first year of operations.

Profit Center

A logical subdivision of the company that is responsible for both sales and costs. Compares to revenue center or cost center.

Usage: The analyst assumed that the Starbucks coffee shop was a profit center for the bookstore.

Promotion

The full variety of communications that a marketer may use in the marketplace.

Usage: The promotion budget included magazine advertising, a website, and pencils with the company logo.

Proprietary Information

Documents and materials prepared by a company that are private and not for public dissemination. Information that would be covered by a non-disclosure agreement (NDA).

Usage: The consultant was asked to sign an NDA before the company would allow access to its proprietary information.

Proxy Statement

A ballot authorizing someone other than the stockholder to vote his or her rights at an annual meeting.

Usage: Nominations for the board of directors are included on the proxy statement.

Q

Quants

People who apply quantitative techniques to investment decisions. Experts in math, physics, and computer science.

Usage: The Wall Street firm was looking for quants to implement its investment strategy.

R

Raising Cash

Selling securities and assets in order to increase the amount of cash in a portfolio.

Usage: The financial advisers suggested that raising cash would be the right thing to do in light of what they expected to happen in the stock market.

Ratio Analysis

A type of quantitative analysis that calculates and compares ratios developed from information on financial statements.

Usage: Ratio analysis makes it possible to compare the performance of large companies with small ones.

Relevant

Adding to the quality of information available for understanding an idea or the choices available.

Usage: Decisions need to be made on the basis of relevant information.

Retained Earnings

The amount by which revenues exceed expenses and dividends paid for a specified period of time.

Usage: When a company experiences a loss, it will have negative retained earnings that year.

Revenue Center

A logical subdivision of a company that is responsible only for sales. Opposite of a cost center.

Usage: The telemarketing division is a revenue center.

Risk

The potential for one or more expected future events to either not take place at all or to occur in some other way than was expected. Also, the possibility of suffering harm or loss.

Usage: Market risk refers to customer behavior; credit risk refers to the potential for default.

Risk And Contingency Plan

An analysis of external and internal events that can jeopardize a project's completion, along with suggested alternative actions.

Usage: By developing risk and contingency plans an organization is prepared to respond to unplanned events.

Risk Tolerance

The ability to manage stress and expectations when the outcome of events is unknown.

Usage: Different people have different levels of risk tolerance when it comes to gambling.

ROI

Return on Investment. Profits divided by the amount invested over a period of time.

Usage: ROI can be used to compare and contrast different investment options.

Runway

The amount of time and resources it takes for a new company to start selling products or services.

Usage: The CEO believed he had eough runway to get the new product launched.

S

Scalable

Able to be quickly increased (as in production), expanded (as in capacity), or upgraded (as in capabilities) to meet demand.

Usage: If the technology isn't scalable, there is a risk that there won't be enough product to meet demand.

SEC

Securities and Exchange Commission. A US federal agency that regulates the securities industry.

Usage: The SEC investigation of the company's officers was front page news.

Selection Criteria

Characteristics that are identified, in advance, as desirable.

Usage: Before purchasing the delivery van for the catering business, they identified two selection criteria: room for five passengers, and good gas mileage.

SOX

Sarbanes-Oxley Act. A US federal law passed in 2002 that set standards for publicly traded companies and public accounting firms.

Usage: SOX requires firms with shares that trade on a stock exchange to provide additional information to shareholders.

SOX Compliance

Adhering to or complying with the rules and requirements of the Sarbanes-Oxley Act (SOX).

Usage: SOX compliance was supposed to increase confidence in the data found in annual reports of companies traded on the stock exchanges.

Spreadsheet

A computer program that is based on a grid-like format and enables automated mathematical calculations.

Usage: Microsoft Excel and Apple Numbers are both examples of spreadsheet software.

Stakeholders

All of those who have an interest in the outcome of a project or a series of events. Includes employees, shareholders, users, customers, and any other group that can be identified.

Usage: The meeting to address the needs of the stakeholders identified all of the competing interests.

Statement Of Cash Flow

A financial statement that reflects how cash is used in an organization.

Usage: A statement of cash flow helps clarify the timing of cash requirements.

Statement Of Financial Position

A financial statement that shows the balances of a company's assets, liabilities, and shareholders' equity as of a certain date. Also called a balance sheet.

Usage: The bank wanted to see the company's statement of financial position before it would approve the loan.

Stats

Statistics. Any collection of quantitative information or data.

Usage: The manager asked for the year-end stats on his performance measures.

Synergy

The working together of two or more things, companies, processes, ideas, or people to create more than what might be expected.

Usage: Synergy is the intangible quality that makes two plus two equal five.

T

Tangible Asset

An asset that is physical in nature and can be seen or touched.

Usage: Inventory and equipment are tangible assets.

Taxable Income

Taxable revenue less all tax-deductible expenses and credits.

Usage: Taxable income is usually different from net income because of tax laws.

Tolerance For Uncertainty

An innate ability to manage even though the facts and events are not yet understood.

Usage: An executive needs a high tolerance for uncertainty, because decisions usually need to be made before all the facts are known.

Top Line

Sales or revenue. Refers to the first line of a profit and loss statement.

Usage: The sales manager was responsible for top line growth.

Tranche

One of a number of securities that are related to the same asset. French for slice, section, series, or portion. Sometimes misspelled as traunch or traunche.

Usage: The first tranche of a sale implies that there will be additional offerings at a later date.

Trust

A business structure in which control of assets and/or property is given to another person or organization (the trustee) that administers the assets for the beneficiary's benefit.

Usage: Sometimes trusts are used as a part of an estate plan to ensure that an elderly parent's money is used for the parent's care.

U

Uncertainty

The state of being doubtful; acknowledgment that the future is unknown. Commonly used when laws, governments, and trends are in flux.

Usage: Stock market commentators frequently claim that uncertainty is the cause when stock prices fall for no specific reason.

Underweight

Circumstance where a portfolio has too little of one asset and is out of balance. Opposite of overweight.

Usage: The analyst said he was underweight bonds or fixed income, suggesting that he would need to purchase more.

V

Valuation

The economic value of a business beyond its revenues and profits. Might be an estimate of what the business would be worth if sold.

Usage: Although revenues were $30M per year, the investment bankers determined that the business valuation was $60M.

Variance

The extent to which a random variable or statistic is dispersed about its mean value.

Usage: The weather reports said the average temperature for the month was 75 plus or minus 5 degrees. The plus or minus 5 degrees is the variance.

Variance Analysis

A comparison of the difference between a budget (expectations) and actual results (what really happened), line by line and section by section.

Usage: A variance analysis seeks to determine whether dollar differences were a result of price changes, productivity changes, or both.

Vested

Protected or established, as by law or right.

Usage: Some employees have to wait five years before their pension benefit is vested.

Volatility

The quality of a price, generally for a stock or security, to widely fluctuate over a short period of time.

Usage: Stock portfolios with a lot of volatility tend to make investors very nervous.

W

Wealth Management

Personal finance for people who are managing high incomes or a significant level of assets.

Usage: Each bank has a different definition of who might be eligible for services from their wealth management department.

Window Dressing

Trading stocks to make sure the quarterly reports reflect a desired portfolio of stocks as compared to the stocks owned between reporting periods. Also refers to the use of accounting tricks.

Usage: The accountants were window dressing so the results would be consistent with the executive's compensation goals.

XYZ

Zero-Based Budget

A budget process where every line item needs to be justified.

Usage: Every five years, instead of a budget based on the previous year's budget, we create a zero-based budget.

www.execuspeakdictionary.com

Because business *is* another language.

Carol Heiberger MBA   Author, Speaker, Educator

www.execuspeakdictionary.com
215-545-1856

www.ingramcontent.com/pod-product-compliance
Lightning Source LLC
Chambersburg PA
CBHW021925170526
45157CB00005B/2193